\<legend\> \</legend\>

Carla Gannis
(images)

+

Justin Petropoulos
(poetry)

Jaded Ibis Press
sustainable literature by digital means™
an imprint of Jaded Ibis Productions

<legend> <legend>

Carla Gannis
(images)
&
Justin Petropoulos
(poetry)

Justin Petropoulos
<legend>

</legend>
<img src = "Carla Gannis">

COPYRIGHTED MATERIAL

© 2013 copyright by Carla Gannis and Justin Petropoulos

First edition. All rights reserved.

ISBN: 978-1-937543-41-9

Library of Congress Control Number: 2013911193

Printed in the United States of America. No part of this book may be used or reproduced in any manner whatsoever without written permission from the publisher, except in the case of brief quotations embodied in critical articles and reviews. For information please email: questions@jadedibisproductions.com

Published by Jaded Ibis Press, *sustainable literature by digital means*™ An imprint of Jaded Ibis Productions, LLC, Seattle, WA USA

Cover design and art by Carla Gannis.

This book is available in multiple editions and formats. Visit our website for more information: jadedibisproductions.com

acknowledgments

We are indebted to Fares Alsuwaidi, Simeon Berry, Loyal Miles, David Ramm, and Sara Jane Stoner for their feedback on this manuscript, as well as N.S. Koenings for gifting us the text from which these poems were sourced. Thanks to Shayna Hawkins, Taezoo Park, Peter Patchen and Eric Rieper, for sharing their incredible talents. Many thanks to the Department of Digital Arts at Pratt Institute, New Jersey City University, and Kelani Nichole and Jereme Mongeon of Transfer Gallery for their support of this project.

Thanks to our parents for their love and support.

Special thanks to Debra Di Blasi and Sam Witt at Jaded Ibis Press for their patience and hard work on the editing and production of this book. Without you we could never have tamed this tentacled beast.

We are grateful to the editors of the following journals for publishing earlier version of these poems:

The Portable Boog Reader 6: "Spooky Action At A Distance" and "Our Telescoping Memory Bias" (formerly "Change Blindness")

The Mantle: "Orders Of Occupation"

Spinning Jenny: "All Balloons Are Runaways"

for the hiveminded

contents

> pedestrian speech acts <   15

> all balloons are runaways <   19

> excavations of the body politic or terra infirma <   29

> spooky action at a distance <   37

> measures of narrative distance <   45

> our telescoping memory bias <   59

> narrativity fact sheet <   69

> orders of occupation <   73

> market accessibility cascades are fragile <   83

> change blindness <   97

> whiteout navigation <   103

> because we go the same places to hide <   113

> flagging procession <   121

> topography from silence <   127

images

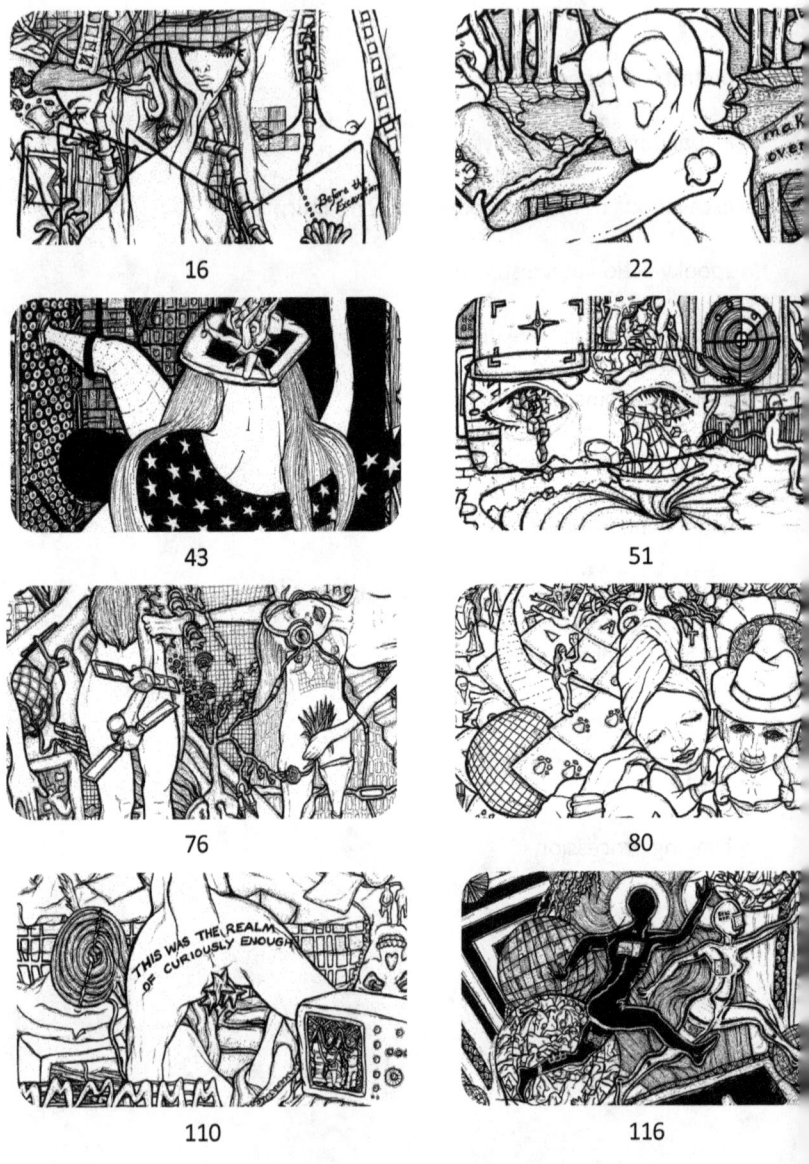

On their backs were vermiculate patterns that were maps of the world in its becoming. Maps and mazes. Of a thing which could not be put back. Not be made right again.

—Cormac McCarthy, *The Road*

This dream is not a map.
A poem is not the territory.

— Harryette Mullen, *Sleeping With The Dictionary*

It is true that the operations of walking on can be traced on city maps in such a way as to transcribe their paths...But these thick or thin curves only refer, like words, to the absence of what has passed by...They allow us to grasp only a relic set in the nowhen of a surface of projection. Itself visible, it has the effect of making invisible the operation that made it possible. These fixations constitute procedures for forgetting. The trace left behind is substituted for the practice. It exhibits the (voracious) property that the geographical system has of being able to transform action into legibility, but in doing so it causes a way of being in the world to be forgotten.

— Michel de Certeau, *The Practice of Everyday Life*

> pedestrian speech acts <

[algorithm]

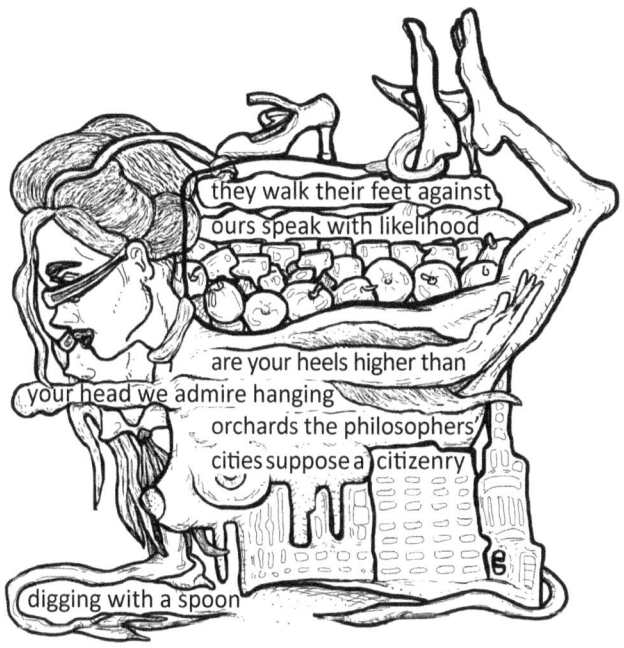

//pedestrian speech acts

evening   that little hatchet   close to   parallel
our dimension   through   which   people passed

the ends   of ladders   each stanza   precedes
the arrival   the pointing   to a time   bird nested

his request of her body   charts   bone mnemonically
parts of it   ladders   tattooed   on his throat

and chest   longing   to order at whose foot
in which welt   each   attended   who interceded

with   the cloud ruler   rain   ties the spruce
it would   be brave not   to say   elegy

but   that was   before   the excavations
rice   wigs   arnica   sad in a cigar   alley

> all balloons are runaways <

[algorithm]

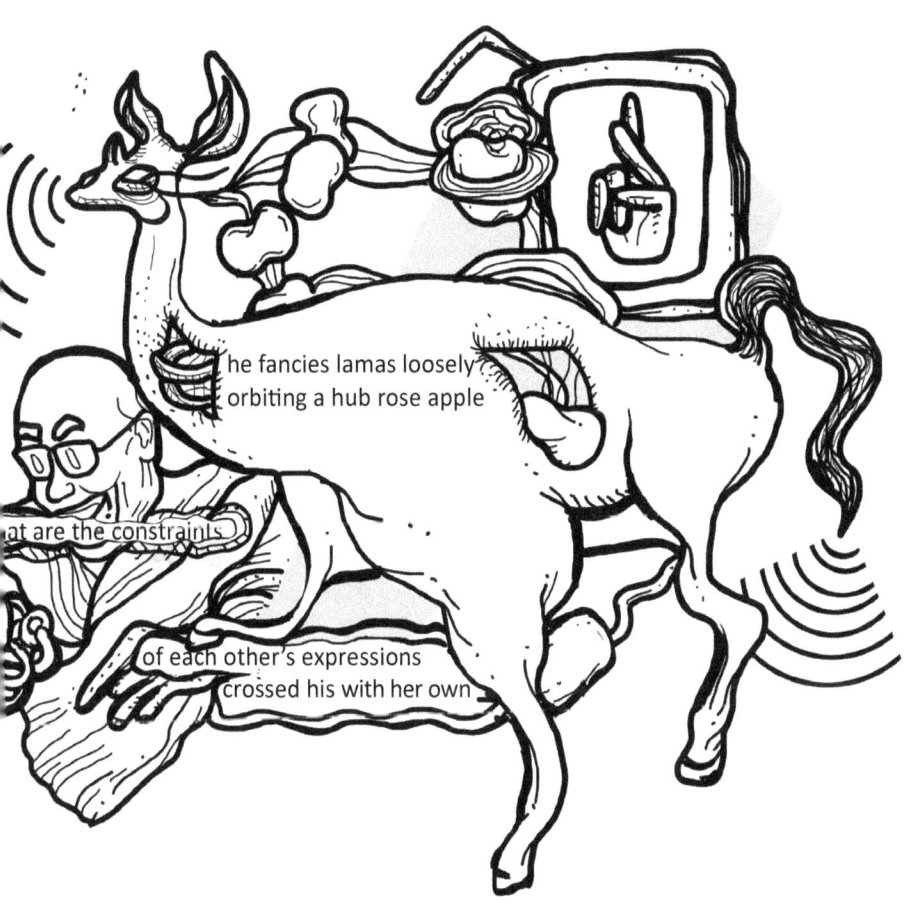

//chorus of idle footsteps

       and   again

                          as far as

we would go
     walk   and
after describing the   circuit

                     colors
             in pairs
                         he
    counted them

        their appointed winters
being past   their

    speech
                            made them
      left them

      living in a small country

//post hoc ergo propter hoc

i leave   continually
                then your food will grow

then he pushed them down under a gopher hill
                spoke   to possess a
                        must not
     wish

who will drive

        another pair
                          tell them

                such and such
a mountain   caused
                      your
     selves   between thumb and finger
     snap   them away

//the place from which proceeds and the nowhere it produces

and when she had given all she
had counted out
 speaking differently
little
 that kind of a country

 wherever passed along never
 a lack of motion

directions where i have been
 nothing is ever finished talking to
you

 stay
when this world becomes bad
 make it over again

//homunculus fallacy

                                          spread
out flat   not stable
this   is all
      by and by   time

        that rope
make it shake
                     until she ceased singing

        walking until he reached the middle of
her   sitting down over across from
                                 her
             ear
                    sounding
        along
         him   to his shoulder
that is as far as they went
that is all   they say

//tiny deportations

        the tango's   foil

faints   neon
                       logia

                              that font

is a peculiarly desolate rendering
      nothing more than

                            symmetry
if water stretching endlessly   bounded

also   the   rose
      it must sink in some unknown

swimming through them   to arrive

//plot driven

                explain the mystery   the   setting
                                    the
idea

                perhaps all   we know
is that in the hour   and in the
hour   has vanished
        the precise   element which
             floated came to be
speculation

        to be a liquid not unlike a narrative

it was   yet not
probably this was an attempt to describe
       the medium

                  thin enough to shape
                  horizons

       like a leaf   and
                would develop roots

//proprioception

                      lotus the water flower
                      and all   lies between

                      that is   be as supple
        as   nevertheless
an anchorage   to something
                      outside itself
        evolving
on   pillars   established
                      an old picture of
the
resting in turn
                      that has awareness

                                of ground

but without   foundation

> excavations of the body politic or terra infirma <

[algorithm]

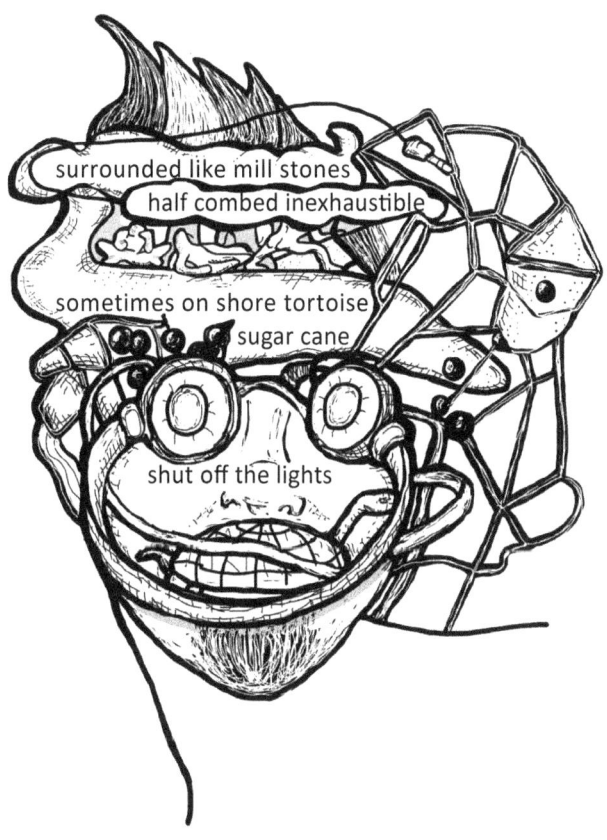

//superposition and the removal of a mass

buried city   an uncovering
of clauses we know   historicity
is fragment and frequency   congregations

nevertheless come dressed for drilling
pictures copied   sacred   a pin inserted
in a pillow   the enforcement engine

at the end of the hailing   and human
remains an inquiry   this vase   its branches
bearing around a drawer of downed bees

how far to the bridge that buckles   someone
follows   that is to say   while those outlines
catalogue foreigners at the forks that reformat

their feet   sink where they suffer
the situation   illness   mercury finds its way

//disposition in conformity with the contours of a pre-existing

into each sketch of sleep   policies
are financed   zenith to nadir   and
reproduced according to polling
at the border   a boy bottles

his diaries   while the cardinals pool
and the darling boxers march   each motion
cycle policed   managed data brackets
the margins   we sit clothed in fictions

fence   shade-tree   dolls folded in a trunk
is that what you're ashamed of   beneath
your trousers   the surveillance
between documents   semblance between

domains   there is static from shareholders
a lowing fever shells each diagnosis

//continuity must be sought or its absence explained

between trousers and your trousers are obvious
nevertheless   costumes compliment any
breakfast   between trees and the tree   however
a correspondence recalled from branches

where the cost of mobile phones   and the price
trend differently depending on who mines
the tantalite   what a delicious name
but under every zipper   a little

bit rot is inevitable   we all lose
our magnetic orientation sometimes
don't we   the borders are obvious shapes
a republic inferred from its bricks   is

tongue the muscle each spectacle waits for
and what verbs   do the viewers use themselves

//between physical contact and being regarded as redundant

the metamorphosis from onion
format   to the duration of a dress

drawn as it rises above orange vases
separated by operators   here

is a little sky   writing on leaves
with soap   the last listeners fossilized

into a staircase   its stability
questionable locality   to interpret

anything we touch   perhaps traffic in
relationships and meanings of compose

their remains   a diagram however
it's possible to sketch largely with no

detail   how a dictionary smells   never
mind the membrane   sleep in your own skin

> spooky action at a distance <

[algorithm]

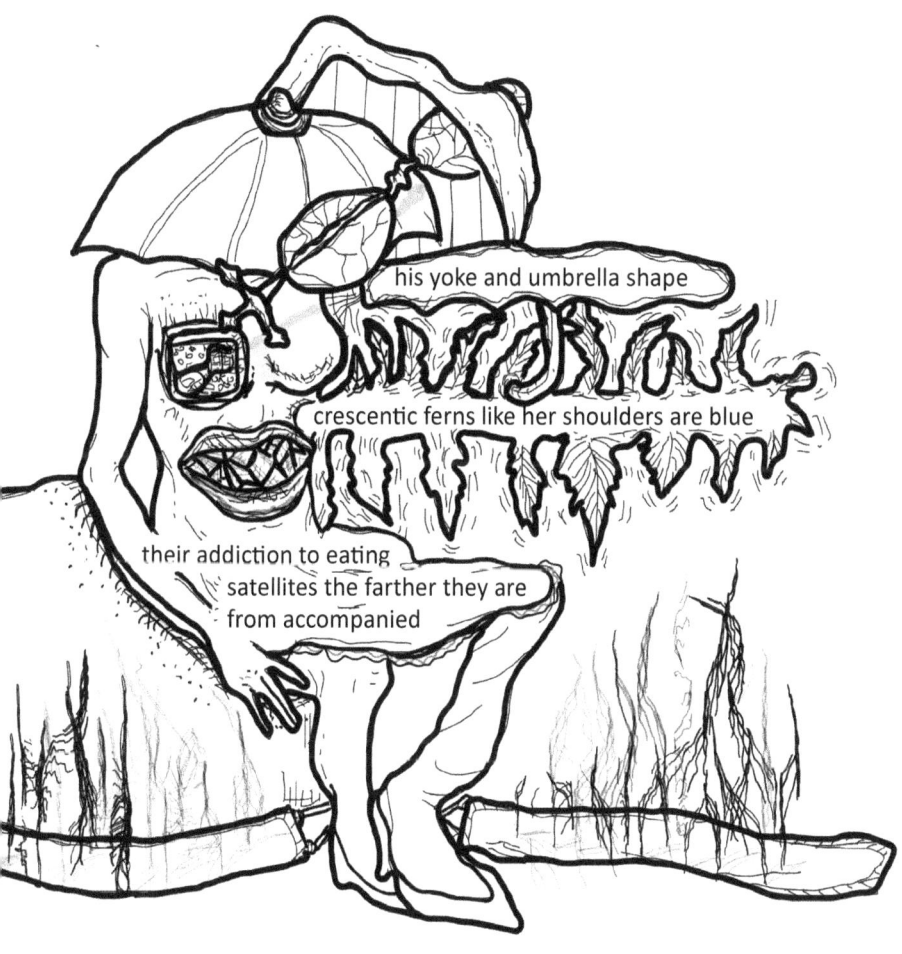

[spooky action at a distance]

coincident with   each   other tradition

however is   not logic   and so disorderly

sometimes   she is powered   with stars

sometimes along   her spine   his ever

after   beneath her   sinking   passed into

the mouth   again at dawn   would take us

too far   this is story   in the

beginning   that stirless   rest   together

was to spring   as   time was   not yet

sing one   word   alone once more   not

yet awake   the wheel and   his   image

concealed in the   vines   but the   day came

a   sun   dials   he slipped   between

the two   hearing   her   spangled body

the extent   her hands   hanging down

remained   violets   without   a struggle

curious   with   out   he has been veiled

in ice   his back   rough   given to   hem

they might   forget   forgetting for a time

between them   air   or ink   circles

roused   with waiting for   answers that never

come   some say   that   heaven answers

to an equation   concealed   under a colossal

gander who   ate the sun   later   in his

turn   catastrophe   recognize it   dream

sodden   staggering breathless   these

two bodies   as   a pair acted upon   beautiful

moving   among   mathematicians

constructed from   interrelated   baffling

fallen   here is   story   separation still

in process   of being made   bodies   collided

terrific   impact   of almonds

torn   from   a body promptly   in   space

and became known   and ever   since

following each   other as   to which   the pursued

which   the pursuer   old   accounts

vary   discourse   tending to prove   that there

may be another   bulwark   her   guess

with similar ones   he says   one   was

terrestrial   she was   inhabited   she

quotes   where the air   is   quiet

this relation   between them she called   the

fable   continually   it meant   nothing else

> measures of narrative distance <

[algorithm]

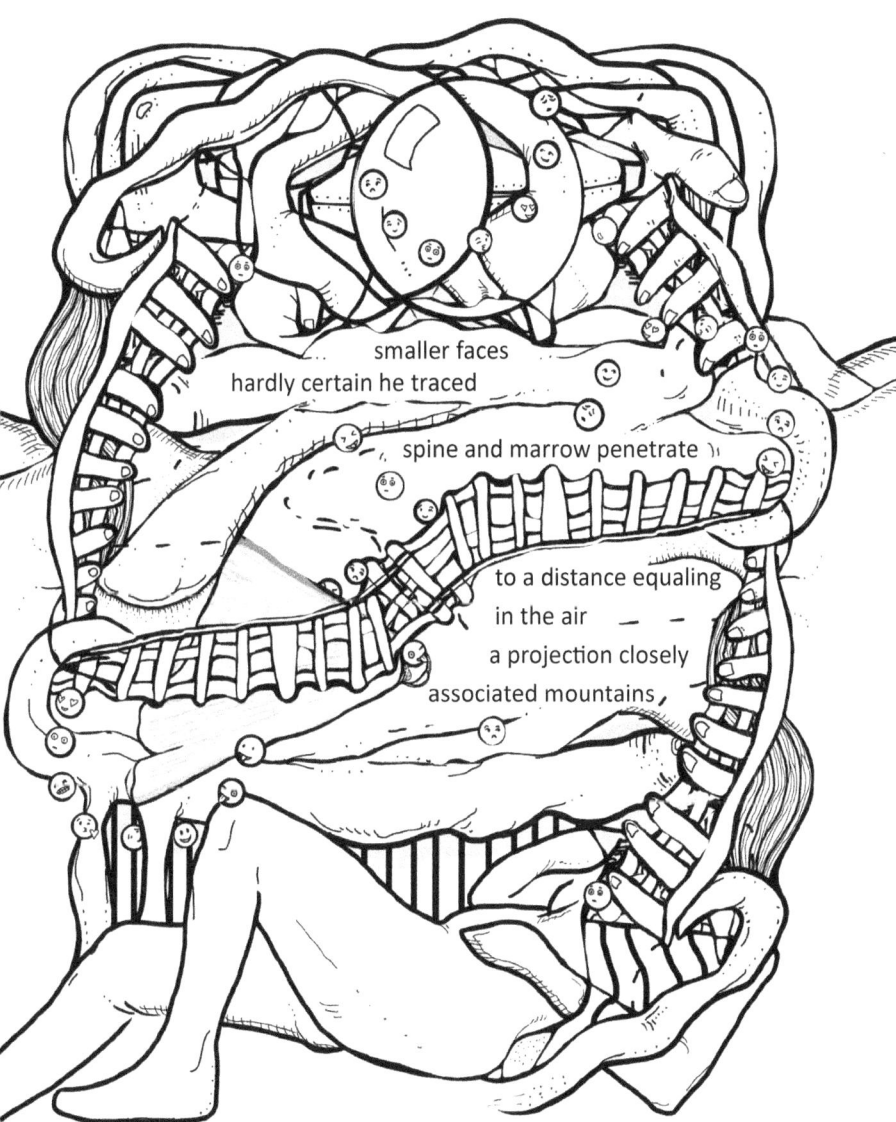

//coordinates of the objective correlative

                regardless the object

        described   minutely

                        how involved
                        she said

                    as mundane as the idea of

     farther
come inside

his collection of distressed

                ships whose cargo was no less
                a dove and

                        traceries

and broken looks

down into a tidal estuary

//coordinates in medias res

she   alters   this place

    lingers
        along its declining
        edge

       for a long time
           after

    fragments
    their

          postures

//coordinates beyond the fourth wall

                                        there would be submissions

                                                  but the fact
                generation does not smile

                              if you have not read it

                                    a few escaped the
                         story

                she has seen him somewhere
           but it is doubtful that anyone

                                        has ever
                                  seen him

                                          reproduced

her hips corner

                      each lie like an anchor

          turning us upside down
will put everything in relation

//coordinates from a quibble

                                                        so many mirages

                  he could not reconcile

                  his present

                                translation

                                                  with sitting
                          under shadows of mountains

.

          to say is to say

                 a little
                 less
                              than nothing

//coordinates with setting

        the canaries are

her only remnants

        conjectural

                                almost across

        this assumption surrounds

                      records riddled

                                with allusions

to vanishied

        people who spoke

                          like varnished

                               pears

    affixed suppositions

he types
        an hypothesis   incorporates

        our traces   as if
            our existence

    proved the explanation

//coordinates deus ex machina

                                                 the lemurian time-cycle explains

          existence mapping only if   existence

                            is a sinking   thing
       we build ships to escape

               gates torrent

                             locality
                             arched like a diver
         always a little scared

                             you might leap through

           the lens

   lose   your
          tiny frame
                             in broken floor

     our outlines
               cut loose from
               fastening

     clouds

//coordinates with paradox

        shadows   they say

            relate
                  fables

i'm telling on you

                        you're a dime
          store

continent   of marshaled
               tin
           all talc

                and hypothetical

                    springs
       identical   except we

                        are threaded
                  together

            differently in time

//coordinates near chekov's gun

every assassin
is assumed
                                    because something has to be

                assumed
                                          among other things

she quotes   the extent of him
boundary
                                          tender
                driven out

        rent

        controlled

//coordinates with a distancing effect

                                                  sown down in
                                                            his mouth

                  her broken   envelope

            fires claimed their victims
                                                why draw

                           analogies
                 after each one

                                              a cord

//coordinates of the unreliable narrator

        because there is   no
        imploring

            radar

         the urge   to glue things

together
             things which   hatch
       escaping

            the way we might

                   inhabit

lost in the silence
of his own
                subroutine

      prove it

            because he remembers

   nothing

     except   the current

> our telescoping memory bias <

[algorithm]

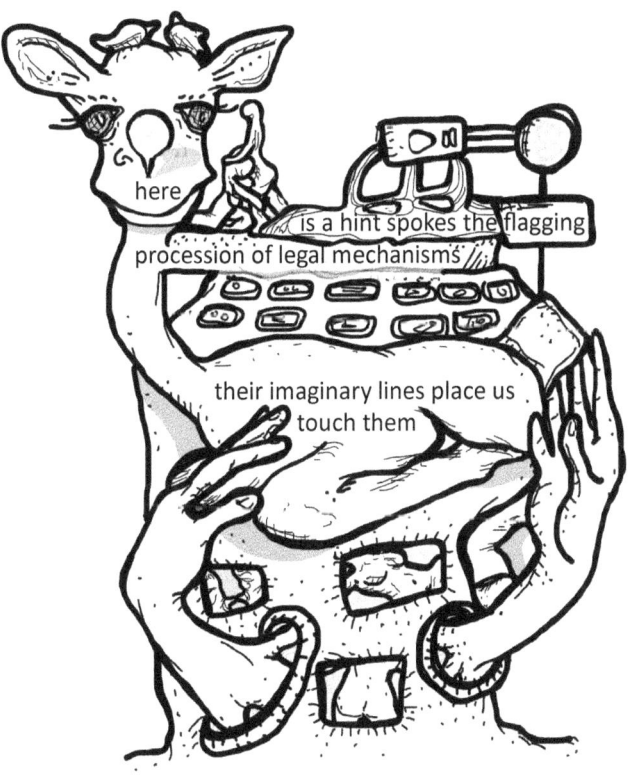

//accessibility hypothesis

                                          pills would dry up and
                we fall down   these liars reason
                      lazy guess   he swam
        complicating systems   mangrove
            tortoise periscopes to surface

                        sometimes in addition
  coiled   floods   when she presses his
                head down   they believe
      they're attached   to heaven   rope
  through their gills   when she changes

                         position his rigging
          moves   sometimes on his back
                         sometimes his horns
    broken   their weight   and so to
              avoid a universe solved

//conveyer belt model

                                                              lariats welter
                                  a foundation dependent
                                            on mythologies
               some lurking concept   shoulders
                               separated by oceans

                                 because he tempted
       a storm   condemned to his head
                  and hands   after the loss
                      he sinuates   fluency
route   fission   her body's stencil

                                quakes if interpret
means wrenched from curious drawings
                             time still occupies
               revolving about it   marked
     her two feet stretch in contrast

                                     to microcosm
                      little epitome   they
                        seem to say   verse
collapse   rose moved between one
                another   pictured under many

                      disguises   hatched beard
                    of stars   perspiration and
                         his parasites   sky
              corresponded to the body
         proof   separated by any

                                  diameter from
    each other   in many fancies
                         they share a giant
                 facsimile   an eyebrow
shaped fog arrives without aid

                    of science   finite
                 figuration possessed by
                     guessing at galaxy
a stratum   confined bed   sounding
          lines throughout our immediate

                     space   seeing as far
              in one direction as an anther
                          she tends toward
                 circular form   an odd method
              it would mean we looked through

                          the proportions of
         their proportions   supposing place
                             or observations
                  are recorded   termites exit
              their rimed limbs   erethismic

//boundary model

however strange
approximate   constellations
looking back he sees
dwindled away   the present
milky   irregular

naturally most
of the early stories are
odd mixtures of clumsy
literalness very close
to divine   ion   sequin

sign   taunting the cliff
motel   her cloned hands
angle the anvil
clouds   conferring acorns   spent
gloves   their vinegar   diode

to a torn saint
or the location of their
discerning was poised
with remotions   ascent
from sensible things   his drawn

numb procession of tin
winged ache   reaching like a spring
the wind tapers
irresistibly   to hem
are you the prism or the noise

that edges through
in this diopter noir
everyone is previous
your thirst   could turn a river
to a startle of straw men

//regression to the mean

                                            warding roads tarred
                         with downed soras   rumor
                                font   divided bodies
                branches   which lose themselves
                        insensibly   habit   flesh

                      these floods   conception
of counter course   seed coat   audit
                                to dwindle into
       paper   data   hew   hawthorn
          timid blue   common answers

                           in a thimble wind
                 accounts of recombining
                       bodies   disposing
of their dawn   wigs   organs groan
               dentin terra   at the end

//prototype

                                          stage built   lighted entrance
                          foreground   a three storied house
                                                      perhaps already
vanished   processions   what people
                         at what time   as boat-shaped

                                            has lost its early
                       significance   people sewn
                                                   into a hollow
                 hemisphere   likewise she rides
                inflated cushions and nothing

                              more safe than her skin
                     on the water   curious
                                relation between
a long time helpless   with two wings
                           and acini phonons

                     fuse to meet her   then
              again that space   he reads her
                    stories   each pin scared
                      riddle   as one does a fish
                  for drying   then he hung up

> narrativity fact sheet <

[algorithm]

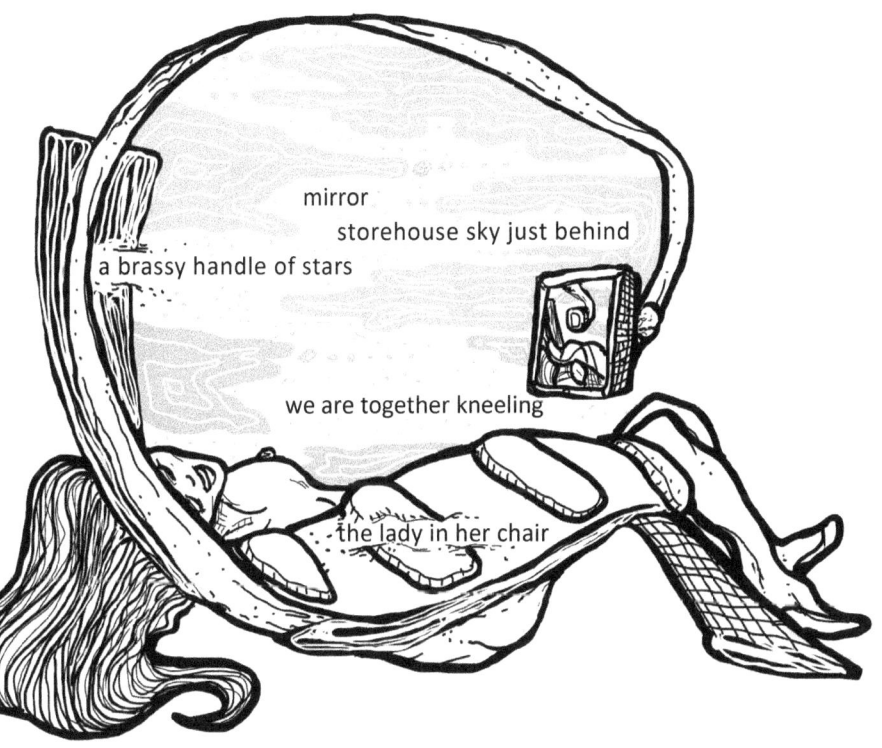

//narrativity fact sheet

      did you know   this
      copy   deflects
           from the original
           but we were source material
           before we ran away
           a reversion to a two party
      system   like veering onto a film
      set   where feathers

      ball the tips of branches
           hidden from parts of time
             close to   or far
      from a humming   bird
      lisps at the light   you
      measure   a climate
      economy   mosaic
           of reconstructed

      correspondences
           patterned in candlesticks
           which circuit   your
      palms   your extremities still
      bound   to description
           agave-leaf thorns
           painted bone   did you
      know they used rubber

      bullets on the crowd   that
      denotation notches   star shaped
           in the pavement
      we walk   our belief   in the
      predicate   case
           any given   given
      voice   swallowed back
           unresolved

> orders of occupation <

[algorithm]

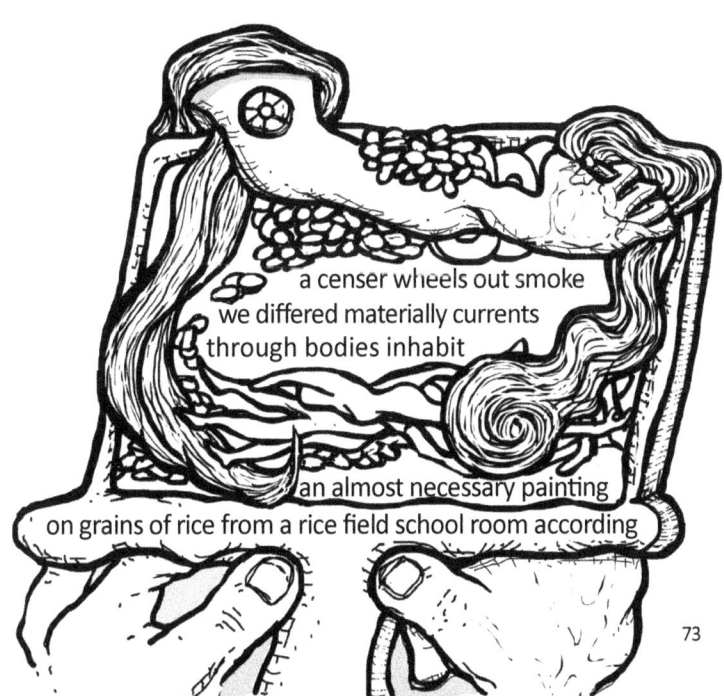

//the disposition of the people

mountains supplied with glacial water in which victims represent the yolk nevertheless windows don't guarantee settlements but demonstrate a problematic thirst in a syntax somewhere between prose and prosthesis they think the souls raised themselves hunt a wide ditch of muddy water while on the other tongue the only means fir tree its bark slippery as the wish to cross is no help left

//subject to uniform proportions

they are stagnant water or the sometimes buildings according to rumor the country of souls is underneath us toward the sunset narrow bridges tracks of people who last went and also tracks of their dogs trail painted ochre hollow enough to hold the piles of clothes brought to her from here letter by letter twilight stationed on each side of the river she was first violin but there were definitely passages she faked

//directions to deliver property

a sweat where he spends most of his time it happens that she succeeds in being a great orator messages limestone or white clay extend ghosts a double row of talk about the newly arrived we use nuance like we say it's my bone algorithm it's not your bone or we say it's our paradox it's not their lighthouse he finds someone standing at the door to greet him call him by name

//the position the rifle is held after

red fescue raspberry canes secure a fence roads obscured burning tires depending on the traveler's legend it appears to have had nothing to do with a special study of the word he says to connote not the or an but simply investment nevertheless a siege or integuments dance from the mist compassing thinly off the lake language rents their bodies displaces its objects

//derivative expressions

moon glosses grape vines white swallows coding themselves into branches she binds his ankles with string literals in the space of flows allegories incorporated applied to a cedar his exported organs at dawn mentioned there described without being heard in the memory and the wind blows it does not blow but I heard it a composite of bodies pendant in the marginalia two birds at our feet release

//a particular economic system

like a satellite a thistle language calculates above us arrives after we are imagined suspended raveling a path back towards a dragnet of makeshift tents it's about evolution but they keep changing the formula for glue he sat on an elephant as it broke she caught them saw to his wonder hat gathering borders impounded footprints opium turnips uniformed rooftops sometimes when it's quiet

> market accessability cascades are fragile <

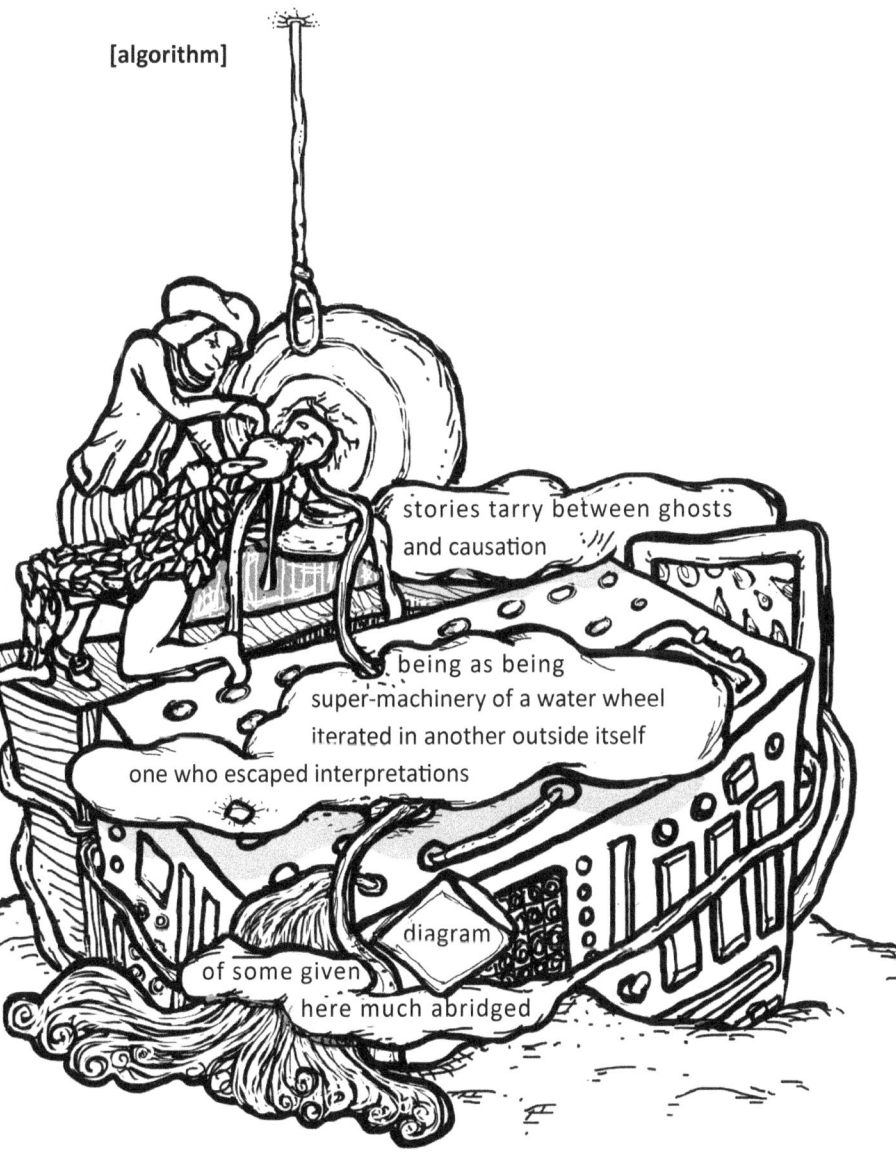

//search

                a single little figure
                taken
                                        then another
     she happens   always by chance
                          a collection
sense of the word
                                  in the gaps
        the search   limited
        what we know
        we know
perhaps believed
                    it would include
diagrams
                        it would gather

//surface]

        weather   true or false
        collection of pictures
                his unhampered body
        the only record
        deliberately brief
                        surface
                        shown dimly
        from the lead   now
                and then blind
                her attempts
        to draw
        bodies   they are surrounded
                similitudes
                    endless questioners
        they are anywhere
                    unanswering
            heaven

//after a fashion

                    born of the speck
                                      in space
                        there is
no equipment
      she never calls
                              no more
than guesses
                  shot into
                  an oblate spheroid

                                of our own
    era   one supplants another
                    and is
                              in its turn
discarded
      sheer pressure
                          questioning
                focused to a point
                exploded
        in space he had been
                after a fashion
      few resources few
                        means

//capacity

       his body   a vague integral
            knowledge of segments
                          he words
                          curious
   the capacity between
          unrelated
          handfuls of means
                his perception
                        faculty for
 story
          continuously dared
               its return
sometimes pure
                       belief composed
          untraceably savage
          spatiality
                  of phenomena
          they resolve   into
                  themselves
certain shapes   superimposed

//orientation

                                circle blossoms
                funeral
                stones everywhere
orientation   tables
of ions build
        the tongue
                motion and its scent
vault   her   acuminated
            body
course impassable
        with pencil and paper
                on a shore raw
with shells
        whatever you will
                                  it will be
                    accident

//walking definite

                    a polygonal figure
                          resolves their unprinted
                                  distance
            curious   dimensions
                    elaborated by
                    birds
filled with compressed air
                walking   definite
                bounding
surfaces   compose
                a perfect series   outside
                      the angular
                test of recurrence
                      a vine or a watch
                spring stretched

//without rungs

                  jacob's ladder   without rungs
                        a rigging
                        of communication
                                  duplicates her position
     that curious struggle
      suggests
                                        is traceable
          curve
                    wreathing of a candle
              tiny   whirl of street
   dust   budding cyclists
                    an onion
                    significant as flight

//appetite

                                                  rations of water
                   years before   the tombs
the struggle between
          analogy
                                            and an appetite
             for limbs   whispered
               from a shell swimming
                   like an upturned basket
          her limits   panting
against a low
                            bound hem

//doctrine

      loose
            this idea   expressed
 by continuous   mountains
 supporting   an unsolved
                sky
                forced to walk
                like flies
     on the opposite ceiling
enclosed in a hollow
                rectangular
   time
        foundation
of measure
            shut the lid
                open umbrella
     chessboard
     the awning of a carriage

//in relief

          i love   you she said
      but what   matters
  about   mountain goats
       is their
                  ambition
            a quantum collapse
        of superpositional
                       memory
      insinuates itself
          into   an economic
model
     cements
              the greatest
       possible surface
             encloses the yolk
                 concave
        convex

> change blindness <

[algorithm]

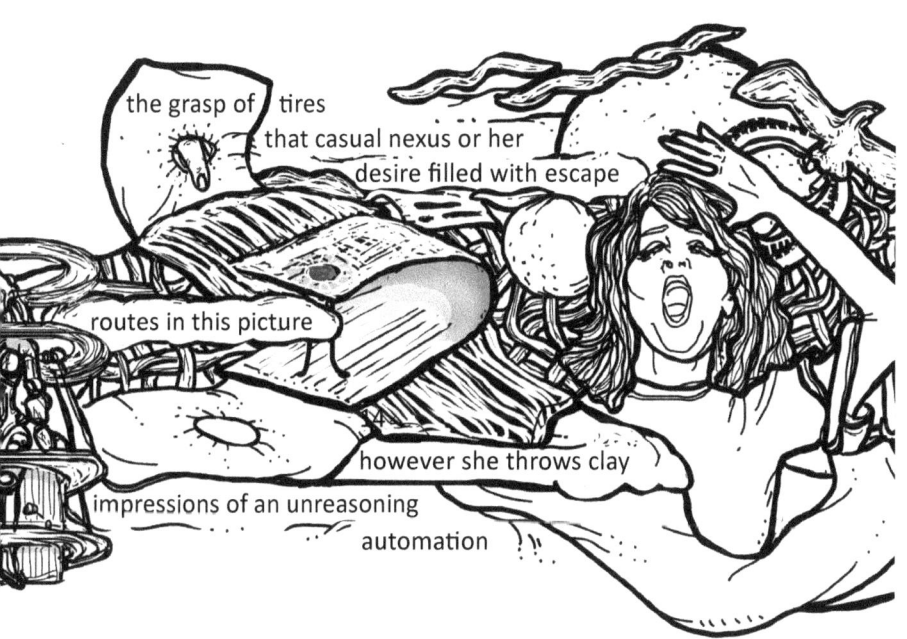

//change blindness

        commerce of moonless voices

                an ellipsoidical
                present thin
                pace of rust

you have really high eyelids
i mean that's the kiss

                we make

a weave of thoroughfares
prosceniums of perverts

                personal prosceniums

she mapped
our conveyances

our habits had their way

        with us

current follows
the precise of course

your hem will hold
us apart

        coast line of terns
        or hands

you made glass
eyes for each of us
too perpendicular

a riven net of beveled bodies
reindexed

                              by a drone
                              error occurred
                              in time

a hen lays an egg

enclosed is its own
accompaniment

recording some sense
of relief

hachure marks
contoured the gentlemen

                                        class

who can explain profit

margins

they were there to be sure
gave you pause

              a broken noun
              rendered just so
              as to occasion

fissures visible by day
however subcutaneous

supposed without a context

              that melting iron
              prices won't impact

a state of continuous export

                    we mingle
                    are then
                    stricken

       from record

> whiteout navigation <

[algorithm]

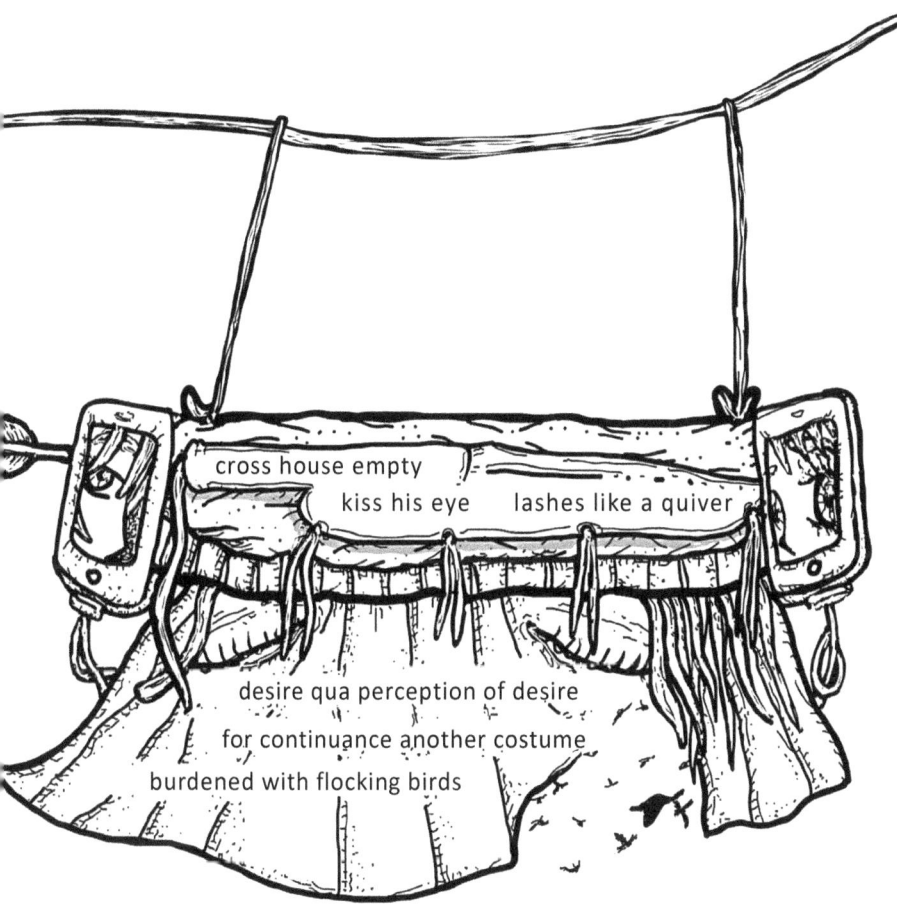

//surviving particle

        half
                        spread out
                        under her
disappeared world
            a surviving particle
survives
                      the conception
      that sky
      is stitched
                                seam
of murmurs
when i was
                  given to
        hollow
interpretations
                  following
sheep
or wanderers
      or watchers

      of lightning
                            in this diagram
            it was really
                         the arrangement
        according   center
the concave side
            of answering
                        shadows

//realm of curiously enough

    i was   relative to you
                                      some distance
beyond the pivot
of a guarded gate
a place   concealed
        takes the place   of itself
                disregarding
                any
                        number of merely
      technical differences
      between them
will serve
                                  as a picture
            a cosmogony
something   quite
other
                    than fragments
text worked
within a period
as she   points
            out   no two
     bears
                any likeness
to this beautiful

// *following data*

        we have   no less
                    than
                    data
                                  following data
              modeled
                translucence
                a table
in the showing
                              ocean
      position   as
      centrifugal
      but he always tasted   swamp

                        sublingual

                                but in
                          the museum
oscilloscope
                soldering iron
                drawing board

     tourists were   bemused

by all the wires

occupied   places
              the   i
                    inhabits
their associated light
                            identical

//corresponding

    he ranged
               above her   or
                        staged
        according to
                                those
                        who built it
               suppose we are
               quadrilateral
                        in particular
                 reeds
                                this one
                        untraceable
                her thighs
                      heave
                fixed stars
                              he
                              listens
        corresponding
                               ions
            arc
            untarred

     his lace
                        regard
proceeds outward
               from objects
                       busy with
       the perhaps
               of occurring

//respective distances

                                that their
            respective
            distances
                                    were not
                            uniform
was already known
                            pass her
        that is
                                            cross a
                              body
                              on every side
                 consider that   sign
                                         stood
                              in the
                                       same
                              relation
                         to this
                         representation
the dents
respectively
                                ants
                          cording
                          tables
their propositions
                          require
       an uninterrupted
       battery

//hemispheres

                              positions
                     of the dead
                                        dotted
                                   half circles
                              corresponding
                     hemispheres
     order
                     cut away
                              to show a system

               the interior
                                        it is to be noted
                              further
                     that the space
     between these   removes
               is almost
                                        the limit of our
                              backward
                     reach
          retracing
                     persistent
                                   recurrences
                                   of some desire
                     or other

//possession

      and so   antedating

                                   possession
         the system
         assumes
                                         diorite
half a   figure
bending a picture
                   bending over
                        doubled

                        strophes
           of time
        consider them
                briefly
                related
left until
                       violent
                separation
       appalling   sink
                            or it
                  may be the
                  third
            point
        of time
                   the sink or again
it   may be two   strophes
                          hiving

> because we go to the same places to hide <

[algorithm]

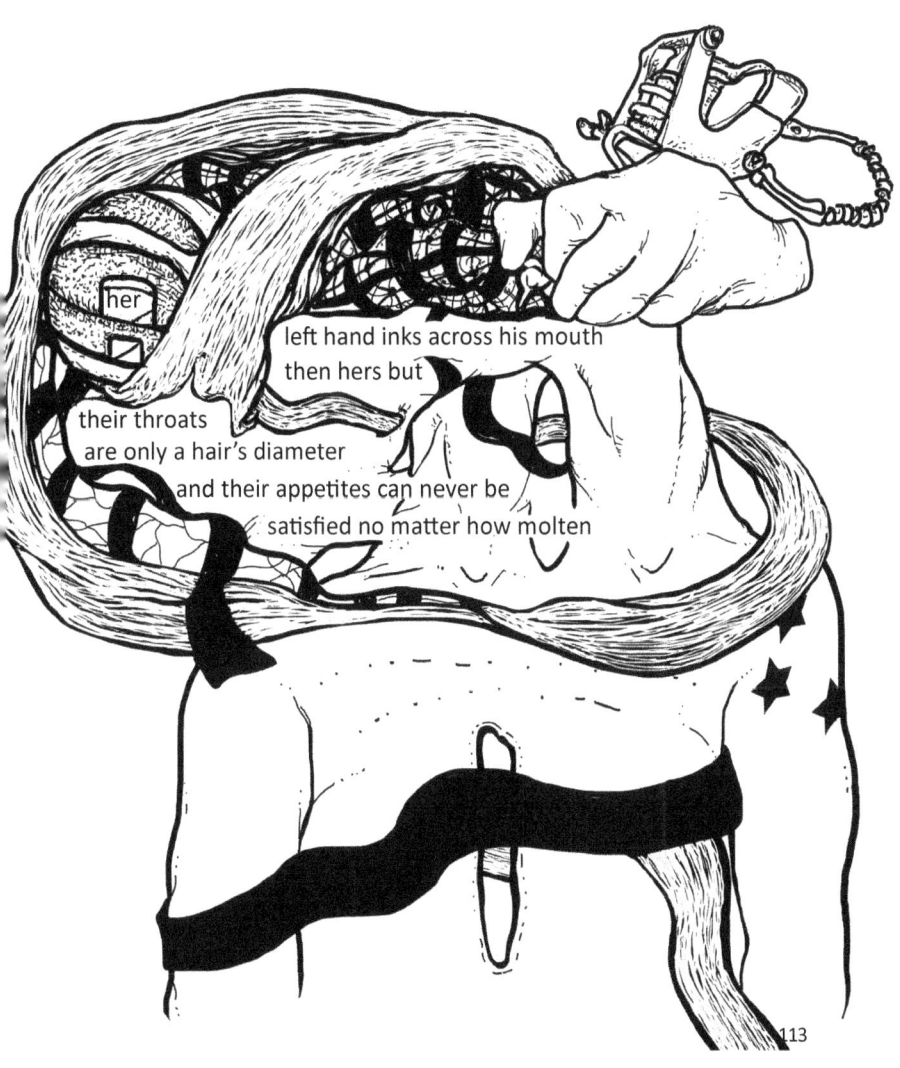

her

left hand inks across his mouth
then hers but

their throats
are only a hair's diameter
and their appetites can never be
satisfied no matter how molten

//travelogue on archival paper

    dormant mirror   yellow
    with its mouse

                            they range
    in time   not to be traced
    in open or secret

                            hatching
    sometimes   an acorn cupped

    white goose   half plunged
    dental   as a theory of two
    centers

                  meaning is what
    we wither into   whither

                        after
    the ophite hissed   escape
    through empty gates
    subjected

                  a delineation
    of the myriad eyed

                        to say
    someone inside out

                        at least
    we know which places
    the bodies are published

//these maps because so casual fill the gaps reasoned for flowers

she eats stems
                         he paces
bed systems   holds her here

associative bearings
of bodies   all that disorder

fled through a rind of eclipse

contractual motion   she pears
instances   heels the limits of
to have held

                 curious
tympana or this hemisphere
rests on nothing but cause
and effect

                 ants distanced
in proportion to intervals
between musical notes

combed with sun

                           she is all
cataracts and shifting clouds

//compass rose

    shells   our velocities
    pressed   cribbed with
    correspondences

                         say we are
    lace-centered   give us an orbit

    to explain another body
    interface always invisible

                         porting
    to reconcile an instrument
    of time   a shadow's cone

    we are separated   slightly
    toward each other

                         obscure
    texts   our hats down scanty
    and corrupt

                  she said nothing
    moves anymore   twists
    herself around his

                  drew
    continents   and pears in pen
    an owl travels until   its edge
    touches shore

                         implicit
                         they build

    out a city's extremities
    from our organs

                         dust
    welds veil   to oracle
    to corroding footstool

//bounding lines carry within them hidden signs

forsake of effect
their appointed
                                         climates

course   photographs
                    her lips reading
his crudely sketched shape

points rearranged   along
a thread   some literal
translations

                              outside
the diagram   they followed us
mingled   ear shaped

perceived as a lack in the signal
differing from fixed

                              morning
is a guess   and hail
is bad for little painted books

cover us   both sides
thin coat of adhesive   while
every interpreter   folds

> flagging procession <

[algorithm]

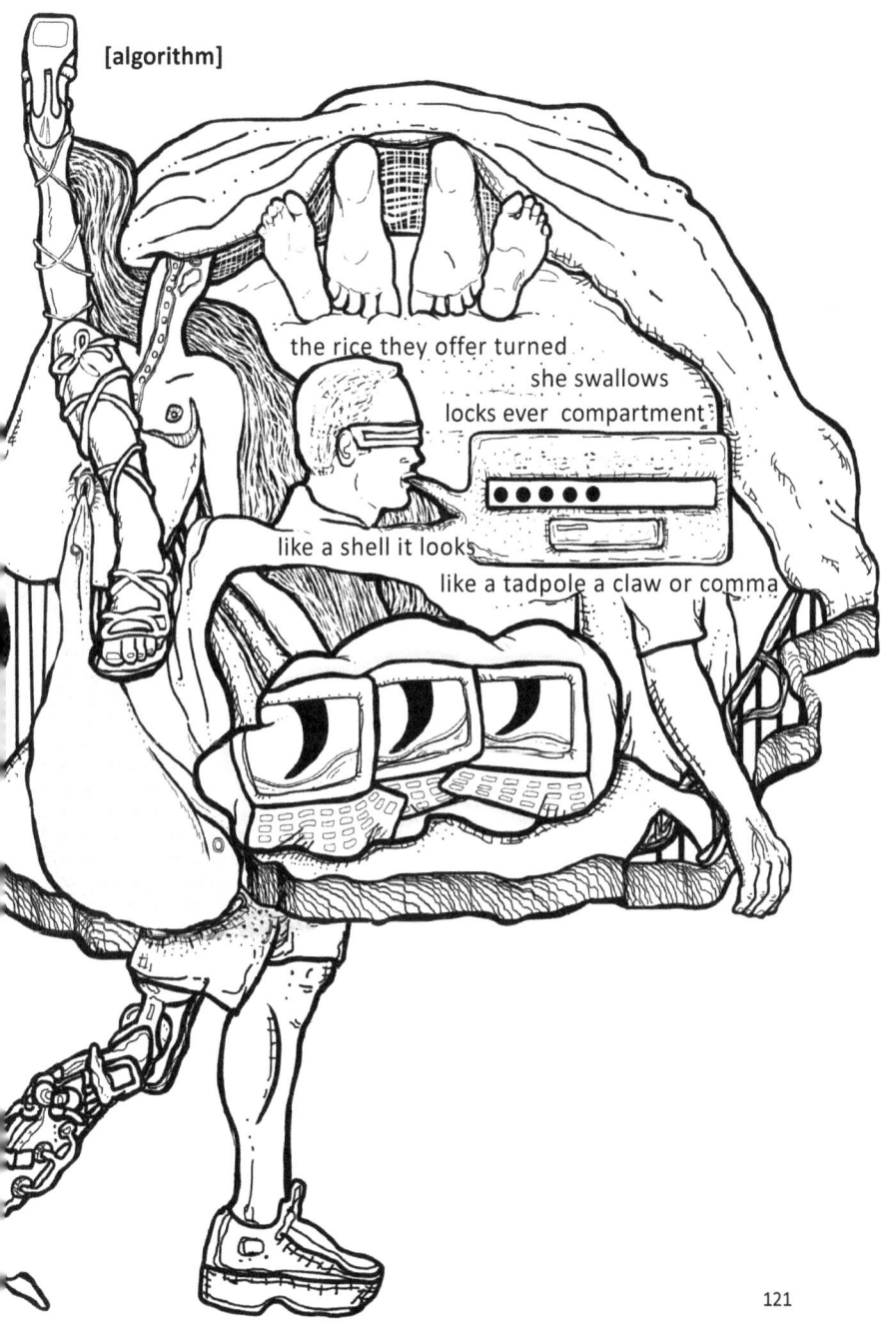

//flagging procession

ashes in the speeches enclosed

in the radio mines dog-headed men suck their food

through these reeds perhaps but we never follow

her travelogue's arrows indicate where

police continue to assert themselves begin to feel

our collars spark from a treadle like a hypothesis

or the span of a trapeze is an autumn of yellow

tornados in a tinderbox pause for the filibuster

but the motion carried every pensioner to pavement

too many empty pillows in our for instances

fistfuls of glances because everyone is a tourist

who interrogates a pawnbroker pencils his torso

with debt as with memory there are many stories

between whose floors we disappear again

pigeons faucet from a tenement window

> topography from silence <

[algorithm]

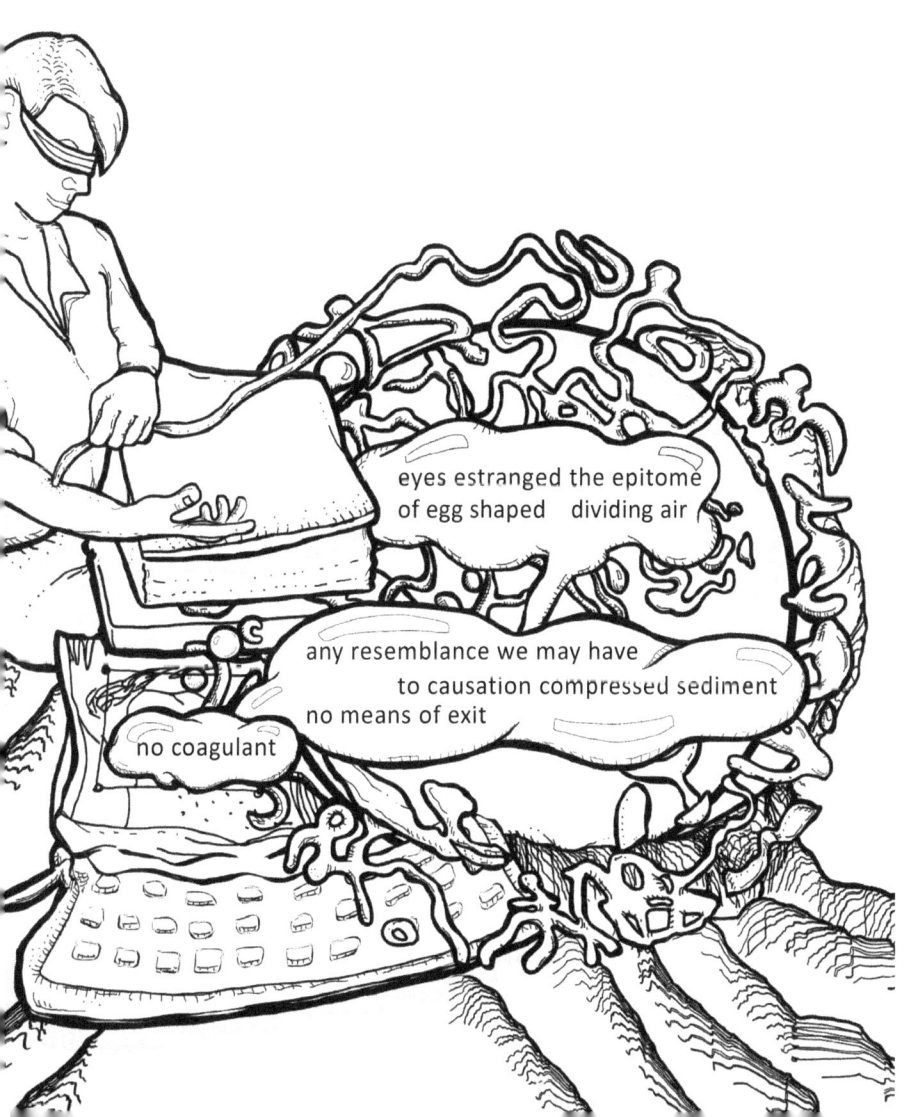

//topography from silence

how many shares
express a workforce
an immigration peculiar
to itself its departures
as incentive a shirt
expressed by a wrist

she has that headache
of liberation what is not
capital has not yet
been determined
but the lemons taste
of carbon and liaisons

in the cargo hold
what is the capacity
of analogy or thin
skinned lemons
for that matter strains
within an outbreak

at a restaurant dimly
populated to be curious
of the space between

stories sometimes
each within the next
tiny harm of streets

bruises your eye
but in revision he is
too familiar to draw
straws with the unknown
operator the oldest
recorded at least

nothing is recognized
as coming from her
practically stripped
of references
refugees comb glyphic
through this space

built on the song bones
of cardinals a belief
that space follows
speech that spectacle
is story is verdict
and feedback victims

of border spending
borrow their sovereignty
against the thatched roofs

of their mouths strangers
on orange bicycles
who tighten the factory

suspension of disbelief
ignore their own
skin that surrounding
fabric incapable of being
the extent of surface
she cannot measure

beyond the limits
of perfect motion
he seemed asleep
without a sound
generating a kind
of consequence

friction beyond
the lines of landlords
is darkness beyond
darling is data
and beyond the last
beyond snow and onions

at the rehearsals
for citizenship
and then soldiers

once again nothing

to eat if somewhere

i can fix it he gave us

the blast mortality

figures so little

has been done

with these pictures

she shows surprise in her

eyebrows we were

covered together

behind the window

a portrait of oblique

lovers scent of holly

of magnetized videotape

and honey that place

still generating prey

for unobstructed speech

but it's an empty shell

without hostages

in the listening position

an extended fog where

it is impossible for us

to speak the ropes

were all stretched

we were tissue
weight remember
what's the matter

when you think about
silence i asked gloves
you said containing
many nurses surrounding
a bell a cyclist in rain
the relief just before

a stranger speaks
your name i know someone
you said who travels
only in that way
as if bodies were not
mixed up with the world

notes on process

The poems and drawings in <legend>   </legend> are based on text redactions of *The Book of Earths*, by Edna Kenton, a compendium of theories on the shape of the Earth and its surrounding folklore.

Most of the sentences from the source text were redacted (blacked-out) with a marker, leaving selected words behind on a page. These words, phrases, and fragments were then organized into poems, some with little or no alteration to the redacted text. Other redacted text was modified through chance and deliberate operations; for example, the use of random word generators, anagrams, or the Oulipo n+7 operation in which each noun is replaced by the word seven places below it in the dictionary. The goal was not only to expand the lexical set available for the poems but also to remap a text and create alternative destinations from Edna Kenton's original language.

The drawings of <legend>   </legend> were created in two media: pen and ink, and digitally. Each drawing is a response to a poem; its style is influenced by the various cartographies presented by Edna Kenton in *The Book of Earths* and images sourced from the Internet.

Each of the book's sections begins with an [algorithm], corollary to the Renaissance convention of prefacing poems with "arguments". Renaissance poetic "arguments" summarized narrative action and acted to guide readers through the poem. The use of "arguments" in poetry during the Renaissance was also a reflection of the literary philosophy of the era, linking poetry and logic. Each [algorithm], like its more narrative predecessor, the "argument", contains the procedure for calculating each poem. Each [algorithm] is a collaborative work composed of text and a drawing, much as poetic "arguments" were presented during the Renaissance. Each [algorithm] drawing was created digitally as both a still image and an animation.

bios

Carla Gannis (@carla_gannis) has exhibited in solo and group art exhibitions nationally and internationally. Her solo exhibitions include "The Multiversal Hippozoonomadon & Prismenagerie" at Pablo's Birthday Gallery, New York, NY; "The Non-Facial Recognition Project" at Edelman Gallery, New York, NY; and "Jezebel" at The Boulder Museum of Art, Boulder, CO. Gannis is the recipient of several awards, including a 2005 New York Foundation for the Arts (NYFA) Grant in Computer Arts, an Emerge 7 Fellowship from the Aljira Art Center, and a Chashama AREA Visual Arts Studio Award. Features on Gannis's work have appeared in *Art Critical, NY Arts Magazine, Animal Magazine,* and *Collezioni Edge*, and her work has been reviewed in *The New York Times, The Los Angeles Times, The Daily News,* and *The Village Voice*. Gannis holds an MFA in Painting from Boston University and is Assistant Chair of Digital Arts at Pratt Institute. She lives in Brooklyn, New York with her partner in crime, poet Justin Petropoulos.

Justin Petropoulos is the author of the poetry collection, *Eminent Domain*, selected by Anne Waldman for the 2010 Marsh Hawk Press Poetry Prize. His poems have appeared in *American Letters & Commentary, Borderlands: Texas Poetry Review, Columbia Poetry Review, Crab Creek Review, Gulf Coast, Mandorla, Portland Review*, and most recently in *Spinning Jenny*. Petropoulos holds an MFA in Creative Writing from Indiana University. He co-curated "Triptych Readings" from 2010 to 2011 and was a guest blogger for Bryant Park's summer poetry reading series, "Word for Word". Currently Petropoulos is the site director of an after-school program for elementary age children and an adjunct faculty member at New Jersey City University. He lives in Brooklyn, New York with his partner in crime, interdisciplinary artist Carla Gannis. Visit him on Twitter at @redactioneer or at Marsh Hawk Press.

www.ingramcontent.com/pod-product-compliance
Lightning Source LLC
Chambersburg PA
CBHW062113080426
42734CB00012B/2846